INDUSTRIAL RAILWAYS
in COLOUR
Scotland
By Adrian Booth

Copyright IRWELL PRESS Ltd.,
ISBN 978-1-906919-46-7
First published in 2012 by Irwell Press Ltd., 59A, High Street, Clophill, Bedfordshire, MK45 4BE
Printed by Konway Press.

For this book (fourth in my *Industrial Railways in Colour* series) attention is turned to Scotland, the country that (in the form of Ayrshire) witnessed early personal memories of BR steam, plus events that were significant in my then-youthful developing interest in industrial railways.

From my home in Yorkshire, I had regularly gone north of the border for holidays since my early teens and, as I was preparing this book, many personal memories came back to mind. Things such as my first-ever visit to Scotland (as a fourteen year old) when train-spotting interests led to my family eating a sandwich lunch beside the Stranraer to Ayr line, where I witnessed the thrilling spectacle of double-headed 'Black 5s' on a northbound passenger train. By the time I was sixteen, I was organising my own tours and recall that the BR Scottish Region was very friendly towards railway enthusiasts and would issue shed permits by the handful to private individuals such as myself, particularly if the week's tour involved purchasing an all-line 'Railrover' ticket. I visited Ayr several times, because I loved watching 'Crabs' working on the local coal trains, and the smokebox plate of 67C's number 42803 looks down on me from my study wall as I type these words. I 'did' all Scotland's remaining steam sheds on those wonderful tours (sleeping in Youth Hostels) and have particularly fond memories of seeing the last J36s in action around Dunfermline and Thornton.

When I was still sixteen I met a Malvern-based railway enthusiast who became a lifelong friend, and it was Robert who introduced me to the Worcester Locomotive Society, whose BR shed bashing tours I joined whenever convenient. The WLS was a forward-looking Society, which began to introduce into its itineraries occasional visits to industrial railway locations. Thus I had already began to dabble with such railways from the age of seventeen or eighteen and started to 'do' local collieries and works around my home patch of South Yorkshire. However, I now recall that it was in Ayrshire, on a WLS tour of Scotland, when industrials really took a grip. The WLS made a visit to the NCB's Waterside system and, after our guide had unlocked the shed, we all trooped inside. Even now, all these years later, I still vividly recall the thrill I experienced as I walked into that warm and smoky shed and saw a group of beautiful black steam locomotives. It was a life changing moment for me, when industrial railways really gelled and became a passionate interest. So Scotland holds special memories for me, and preparing this book has been a very enjoyable experience.

All my pictures were taken on Agfa roll film colour transparencies (2¼ inch square) using a series of Yashica cameras. To pinpoint the locations depicted herein, various geographical notes on roads and railways have been provided. The road numbers are modern (to aid location on current maps) although were not necessarily so designated at the time I drove along them. I hope that readers will enjoy my fourth selection of industrial railway colour pictures and I feel that there may just be a fifth and final book in me (if Irwell are in agreement) to complete the series. For anyone unaware of the previous three books they are *Industrial Railways in Colour* (general coverage of the whole UK), *Industrial Railways in Colour – Yorkshire* (covering purely the White Rose county) and *Industrial Railways in Colour – South Wales* (covering the area south of the Heads of the Valleys road).

Adrian Booth, Rotherham, South Yorkshire

Our look at the industrial railways of Scotland will form a clockwise tour beginning in the south west of the country, which was how the author's trips were nearly always planned. At least one visit was made to Scotland every year, with the trip that was made with friends always known as the 'Annual Scottish Bash'. For many years this involved an overnight stay in Carlisle, before venturing across the border and visiting some of the narrow gauge peat bog systems around Eastriggs. A few miles further west along the B721 minor road was the coastal village of Powfoot, near Annan, where the Nobels Explosives Company had a factory. Standing in the yard on 1 July 1975 was Hawthorn Leslie W/No.2859 of 1911, an 0-4-0 saddle tank that had previously worked at the company's Grangeston Works, near Girvan. It was fitted with 12in x 18in outside cylinders and 3ft 0½in diameter wheels.

A typical trip would involve a visit to the lovely town of Dumfries, where visits to a bakery shop and the BR shed would precede a drive up the A713, passing Loch Doon and the old town of Dalmellington, to arrive at Waterside. This isolated hamlet originally grew up due to the emergence of the Dalmellington Iron Company (DICo), which exploited the massive local deposits of coal and iron, and also turned its hand to brick making. On 29 May 1978 a careful climb to the top of a giant slag tip produced a panoramic view of the former DICo site, which by then was owned by the National Coal Board (NCB). Abandoned brick kilns stand in front of the chimney, while the second building from the right is the locomotive shed, mentioned in the Introduction. In the foreground English Electric Bo-Bos numbers 20120 and 20091 double head a train of 16-ton mineral wagons, carrying freshly hewn Ayrshire coal down the single track BR branch line to Ayr Harbour sidings.

The Dalmellington Iron Company's site was later operated by the NCB. The site became the headquarters of the large NCB Waterside operation that included offices, a locomotive shed, locomotive repair workshops, wagon works, and a coal preparation plant. The latter (named Dunaskin) processed coal that was brought in from nearby mines that are described in greater detail in later captions. Here we have a view taken inside Waterside's four-road locomotive shed, a structure built of red brick at its base with Perspex windows and corrugated sheeting wall tops and roof. Standing inside on 17th May 1977 is 0-4-0 saddle tank No.1 (Andrew Barclay W/No.2368 of 1955) which was fitted with 16in x 24in outside cylinders and is in green livery. The wheels display evidence of possible swapping around, as the leading pair are painted red, whilst the rear ones are black.

Dunaskin Coal Preparation Plant had a double wagon tippler at the east end of the yard, seen here in action on 29 May 1978. Rakes of loaded internal user coal wagons, brought in from Minnivey and Pennyvenie collieries, were positioned on the roads leading to the tipplers, to where they were lowered individually, being controlled by shunters. The mechanism for each tippler involved a steel rope passing over a wheel (seen top right) which was drawn in to lift the platform into the tipping position. The coal was fed into the washery via a sloping conveyor visible in the left background and, after washing and screening, was loaded into steel-built mineral wagons that had been lowered by gravity into the screens. A steam locomotive collected the fulls at the low side of the washery, and ran them to Cutler Sidings for collection by BR – to be taken down to Ayr as seen in the earlier photograph of the pair of Class 20s. A wooden six-plank wagon (right) waits to be emptied.

When the wooden internal user wagons had been emptied, they were collected by the steam yard pilot and marshalled into rakes to await transporting back to the outlying collieries. 0-6-0 side tank locomotives normally handled these runs but, on a visit of 15th August 1972, a rake was in the hands of two 0-4-0 saddle tanks. These were No.10 (Andrew Barclay W/No.2244 of 1947) and No.19 (Andrew Barclay W/No.1614 of 1918) both fitted with 16in x 24in outside cylinders. The author and his three friends were invited to have a ride and were placed in the supplementary coal tender coupled to No.18. The quartet recall sitting in the tender, with smuts raining down on their heads as the train chugged through the Ayrshire countryside, but also the chagrin of a line side photographer who had lined up a master shot of the double-header at Minnivey loop – only to see four grimy gricers spoiling his picture!

The Waterside railway system previously operated to other collieries but, by the 1970s, had been cut back to serve just Laight Spoil Tip, Minnivey Colliery and Pennyvenie Colliery. A single track 'main line' railway ran out of Waterside, heading in a generally easterly direction, and the first stage of the line is seen in this view taken on 17 May 1977. The Waterside site is visible in the right background (marked by the chimneys) whilst the massive slag tip (from which the Class 20s were photographed) is seen in the background immediately to the right of the locomotive's exhaust. In charge of the rake of internal user wooden wagons is 0-6-0 side tank No.17 (Andrew Barclay 1338 of 1913) which was the author's personal favourite locomotive on the system. This 64 year old gem was fitted with 18in x 24in outside cylinders and 3ft 9in diameter wheels. It was heading out to Minnivey Colliery.

At Dunaskin Washery, spoil wagons normally stood on the track which is just visible on the extreme right of the earlier view of the tippler. These wagons were steel built side tippers, which were positioned beneath a chute that fed into them the washery spoil. When a rake was ready, these fulls were collected by a steam locomotive and hauled along the main line to Laight, roughly one mile east of the washery. At this point the locomotive ran its train past a set of trailing points and then pushed the rake up a sharp gradient on to the tip. The crew then braked the locomotive and dismounted, before walking along the rake and operating the tipping mechanism on each wagon in turn, until all had been emptied. The locomotive then propelled the empties back to Dunaskin Washery, as in this view of No.24 (Andrew Barclay 2335 of 1953) with its crew of four men on 31 May 1976.

Minnivey Colliery was located approximately 2½ miles east of Waterside at the hamlet of Burnton, just to the north of the town of Dalmellington. The colliery was opened by the NCB in 1956 on the site of the DICo's former Burnton Washery, and Waterside locomotives collected its coal which was run down to Dunaskin Coal Preparation Plant. After the author and his three friends had enjoyed their ride in the coal tender on 15 August 1972, 0-4-0 saddle tank No.19 (Andrew Barclay W/No. 1614 of 1918) was standing in the yard during a break in shunting manoeuvres. This superb little locomotive was acquired new by the DICo and later passed to the NCB, whose long obsolete 'West Ayr Area' lettering it still carried. It was withdrawn by 1978 and was later preserved at the Scottish Industrial Railway Centre – an organisation that took over the Minnivey Colliery site after its closure and turned it into a preservation site. No.19 is still with the SIRC.

Trains which were approaching Minnivey Colliery from Waterside negotiated Minnivey loop which was out in the rolling Ayrshire countryside. 0-4-0 saddle tank No.10 (Andrew Barclay W/No.2244 of 1947, with a good head of steam) was shunting a rake of ten wooden wagons there on 15 August 1972 (shortly after the author's ride) with No.19 in action in the right background. The locomotive water supply tank can be seen in the background, just to the right of the tree. No.10 was transferred to Killoch Colliery, Ayrshire, in 1975, and withdrawn by 1978, later being preserved at the Scottish Industrial Railway Centre at the site of Minnivey Colliery. No.10 is still with the SIRC, an organisation that had no less than three dozen locomotives (of three different gauges) as at 1 January 2006.

No.24 was the last steam locomotive purchased new for the Waterside railway (in 1953), and cost just over £10,000. It was acquired principally to work 'main line' traffic to Pennyvenie Colliery, which the NCB intended to increasingly exploit. No.24 was another of the 18in x 24in outside cylinder 0-6-0 side tank design which had proved to be so efficient at Waterside, but it got off to a bad start, with its drivers claiming that it was a bad steamer. This continued until 1965 when the NCB chose No.24 among a small number of locomotives to be experimentally fitted with the then new Giesl ejector, which was claimed to reduce coal consumption. Men from Andrew Barclay fitted the device and the locomotive was positively transformed, running with the giesl for the rest of its career. The giesl is clearly seen in this view dated 1 July 1975, taken at Minnivey Colliery.

From Minnivey Colliery, the NCB single track 'main line' ran in a generally easterly direction, passing the north end of Dalmellington, towards Pennyvenie Colliery. Minnivey Colliery was one of the last two to remain open on the system but, when it closed in November 1975, it left just Pennyvenie operational. In happier times, on 15 August 1972, 0-4-0 saddle tank No.19 (Andrew Barclay W/No.1614 of 1918 with plenty of steam to spare) storms towards Minnivey with a rake of wooden wagons from Pennyvenie Colliery. Minnivey Colliery was the location of a large NCB canteen and on many occasions the author used these facilities. A particularly fond memory is once going out into the cold Ayrshire countryside at 6am for a two hour photographic stint in the crisp, cool air, before retiring to Minnivey canteen for a pint mug of red hot NCB tea and a couple of mouth watering bacon butties!

Pennyvenie Colliery was roughly one and a quarter miles east of Minnivey and marked the end of the Waterside system. The pit was situated alongside the B741 minor road that ran north east from Dalmellington to New Cumnock. For many years the colliery had a fine Marshall Fleming of Motherwell vertical boiler steam crane parked in the sidings. When word circulated that Pennyvenie Colliery was to close on 6 July 1978, numerous enthusiasts who were eager to take their last pictures visited the system. The author travelled up from Yorkshire to Ayrshire, to pay his own last respects, and spent two days on the system, experiencing mixed emotions: the joy of watching No.24 in action in lovely sunny weather, but tinged with nostalgia, sadness and disbelief that it was for the last time. No.24 is seen in the pit yard at Pennyvenie on 30 May 1978 with a rake of the system's characteristic red wooden wagons.

Approximately ten miles due east of Ayr, along the A70 road, was Killoch Colliery, situated right alongside the main road. The colliery's coal was dispatched by means of a meandering three miles long branch to Drongan, and thence via a BR branch up to Annbank and westwards to Ayr. Sinking of Killoch Colliery by the NCB commenced in December 1952 and the pit opened about 1959. Its relatively modern industrial architecture is evident in this view of 29 May 1978, at which time the pit was stated to employ over two thousand men. On this date a tour of the colliery's surface 3ft 6in gauge tramway revealed a fleet of four 4-wheel diesel mechanical locomotives, all constructed by Ruston & Hornsby of Lincoln. W/No.256273 of 1948 (which arrived from Rothes Colliery about 1967) was a 48hp machine, and is seen shunting tubs that were being loaded with timber for lowering underground.

On the same visit to Killoch Colliery, on 29 May 1978, the internal standard gauge railway had a roster of four diesel locomotives. All were of 0-4-0 wheel configuration, and comprised mechanical, electric and hydraulic transmission systems. The hydraulic locomotive was originally a member of the unsuccessful 225hp class (D2708-80) which worked on the BR Scottish Region. D2738 (North British W/No.27833 of 1958, pictured here) entered service in November 1958 allocated to 65G Yoker shed and, after a short life, was withdrawn from Eastfield shed in June 1967. It went to Andrew Barclay's works at Kilmarnock in October 1967 and, after a rebuild, emerged in 1969 and moved to the NCB's Killoch Colliery. It worked longer for the NCB than it did for BR, but was scrapped by Alex Smith Metals of Ayr in January 1980.

Two miles further east along the A70 was Ochiltree and, one and a half miles north east of there, was Barony Colliery. This pit was sunk in 1906-12 by the old firm of William Baird & Co Ltd and linked to the main line by a half-mile branch running north from the pit to join the Kilmarnock to Dumfries line. In charge of traffic on 1 June 1976 was 0-4-0 saddle tank No.16 (Andrew Barclay W/No.1116 of 1910) which was fitted with 16in x 24in outside cylinders. In ever deteriorating weather conditions, No.19 was using every ounce of its power to pull five loaded merry-go-round wagons up a slight gradient on greasy rails. At barely crawling pace, plumes of exhaust belched out of No.19's chimney as cinders from the firebox cascaded down between the tracks. It barely made it past the author (whose boots were caked in thick black slurry) before a violent rainstorm erupted.

Andrew Barclay W/No.1116 of 1910 was transferred from Mauchline Colliery to Barony Colliery on 20 August 1974. It worked at the latter for a while, as seen in the previous photograph, before being placed on standby status as diesel locomotives did all the shunting. It is seen on 10 June 1981, standing on a rusty and weed covered siding, in the company of a fellow Andrew Barclay 0-4-0 saddle tank. Just visible behind, the latter is No.9 (W/No.2369 of 1955) fitted with 16in x 24in outside cylinders. Also in the background can be seen the cooling towers of the neighbouring Barony Power Station. Barony Colliery was one of the few UK pits to retain steam locomotives into the 1980s, but the internal railway system fell into disuse, the rail connection was removed with effect from 25 May 1986, and the colliery itself closed in 1989.

The South of Scotland Electricity Board operated Barony Power Station. It was built as an experimental power station, designed to burn in its boilers slurry obtained from various Ayrshire collieries. The experiment proved to be a great success, and the power station burned slurry brought in from collieries including Barony, Killoch, Knockshinnoch Castle, Mauchline, and Pennyvenie. On 10 June 1981 there was a large stockpile of slurry at the adjacent Barony Colliery, while deliveries were still being accepted from Killoch Colliery – although the other pits by then had closed. The coal plant is seen in this view, with 0-4-0 diesel hydraulic No.7 (Andrew Barclay W/No.516 of 1966) engaged in shunting a rake of 16 ton mineral wagons. No.7 formerly worked at Clyde's Mill Power Station at Cambuslang, and was fitted with a Cummins diesel engine and Westinghouse air equipment.

Continuing eastwards along the A70 road from Ochiltree, the road swings in a north easterly direction beyond Cumnock and Lugar, to soon arrive at Cronberry. A mile beyond here was Cairnhill Colliery, at the end of a rural branch line that diverted off the BR Ayr to Muirkirk main line at Auchinleck. Cairnhill Colliery was opened by the NCB in 1954 and the use of locomotives commenced in 1960. Entry to the mine was by means of a minor road that turned off the A70 at the intriguingly named Gasswater, and the internal line out of the colliery crossed this minor road on the level. On 1 June 1976, the road provided the vantage point to photograph 0-4-0 saddle tank No.1 (Andrew Barclay W/No.2368 of 1955) propelling a rake of seven 16 ton mineral wagons towards the colliery. No.1 was fitted with 16in x 24in outside cylinders, and had arrived at Cairnhill Colliery from nearby Lugar in June 1965.

Continuing further northeast along the A70 road from Cairnhill brings you to Douglas Water, where Peat Development Ltd once worked a peat bog. The company used two 'Simplex' 4-wheel diesel mechanical locomotives and, on 10 June 1981, Motor Rail W/No.7066 is seen on the 2ft gauge. The operating system was quite fascinating! A rake of wooden 5-plank wagons is in the background, wheels spragged on the gradient. The first wagon was attached to the locomotive, which pulled it a few yards to get it moving, whereupon a second man deftly uncoupled it, and the locomotive speeded off round the bend. It diverted into a siding, the brakes were applied, and the driver jumped off and swiftly changed the points. Meanwhile, the wagon followed round the bend, controlled by the second man, who was then joined by the driver. Both men then dug their heels into the ground, to act as a brake, to halt the wagon at the tipping point. After all wagons had been similarly dealt with, the rake was trundled back to the moss for re-filling.

After the delights of the narrow gauge, retracing your steps back towards Ochiltree brings you to the northbound A76 road. This passes through Mauchline (famous for its transfer-printed varnished boxwood souvenir ware) to arrive in the large town of Kilmarnock, which at one time had steam shed 67B Hurlford on its outskirts. Here was the Caledonia Works of Andrew Barclay, Sons & Co Ltd, the prolific locomotive builder whose products are featured throughout this book. When visited on 30 May 1978, the works shunter was a very unusual locomotive. Hunslet W/No.5306 of 1958 was a member of the maker's 'Yardmaster' class, designed for one man operation in small yards, and which could be driven from either side platform or from inside the cab. When built, 5306 was fitted with a Dorman type 4LB engine rated at 71hp and a two-speed mechanical gearbox. Only a small number were ever built, which made 5306 a very rare machine.

Moving inside the Andrew Barclay workshops on 30 May 1978 revealed seven brand new 90hp narrow gauge underground locomotives under construction, plus two standard gauge 0-4-0 diesel hydraulics undergoing major overhauls. The latter are illustrated here, with two men busily engaged on attending to the front locomotive's engine. The pair comprises North British Locomotive Company W/Nos.27646 and 27647 of 1959, originally built under the maker's internal order number L71 for the Ministry of Supply, who specified they should have "provision for arctic and tropical operation"! When new they were fitted with National type M4AAU5 engines rated at 275hp and allocated WD running numbers 8209-13. The Ministry of Defence clearly had a higher opinion of its North British shunters than did BR of its D27XX class (see earlier) and were happy to pay for expensive overhauls for nineteen year old locomotives.

Heading due west out of Kilmarnock brings you to the Ayrshire coast and the small town of Ardrossan, which was served by the Ayr to Greenock main line. The author first visited on 24 August 1969, when the cavernous four-road BR steam shed (67D) was obviously devoid of steam but held five class 08 diesel shunters. When revisited on 17 May 1977, however, the town was again host to steam motive power. The Shell Refinery utilised an 0-4-0 fireless locomotive (Andrew Barclay W/No.1952 of 1928), a type characterised by having outside cylinders fitted underneath the cab. The type did not have a conventional firebox fed by coal but, simply put, the fireless locomotive's 'boiler' was actually a pressurised reservoir that was charged with water and steam. The driver drew steam out of the reservoir to work the cylinders until a fall in water level – with a gradual fall in tractive effort – required a return to the charging point for a top-up of steam.

The Glengarnock Iron & Steel Works was established in the mid nineteenth century, in a rural location close to Loch Kilbirnie in west Ayrshire. It had a railway connection onto the Ayr to Glasgow main line. The works was an early convert to diesels, scrapping the remnants of its steam fleet by the late 1960s, having purchased three John Fowler diesel mechanicals and eight Ruston & Hornsby diesel electrics between 1952-60. Further modernisation of the fleet saw diesel hydraulics arriving in the mid 1970s and, on 18 August 1980, number DH11 (Andrew Barclay W/No.602 of 1975) was shunting three wagons over the weighbridge. Ex works on 4 November 1975, the 0-4-0 was fitted with a 252hp Cummings engine. The driver takes time out to discuss the next shunt with the weigh man, as DH9 (Hunslet W/No.7046 of 1971) revs up outside the locomotive shed in the background.

Continuing north eastwards along the railway, and the parallel A737 road, brings you to the western suburbs of Glasgow. In Renfrew was the works of Babcock & Wilcox Ltd, a firm of boiler makers which had operated there from the late nineteenth century. This firm obtained its first shunting locomotive (an Andrew Barclay 0-4-0 saddle tank) in 1896 and utilised ten steamers over the years, although dispensing with this form of motive power immediately after World War 2. Thereafter the internal railway was dieselised with the acquisition of seven Ruston & Hornsby 4-wheel diesel mechanical locomotives in 1946-47, plus two 0-4-0 diesel electrics from the same builder in 1951. One of the earlier type is seen here on 17 August 1970. A member of the maker's class 88DS, number P.4937 (W/No.245034, ex-works on 29 August 1947) was fitted with a Ruston 88hp engine, four speed gearbox and final drive by roller chains.

Moving in an anti-clockwise direction around the suburbs of Glasgow brings you to Cambuslang, to the south east of the city centre. Here the British Electricity Authority (until 1954) and subsequently the South of Scotland Electricity Board operated the Clyde's Mill Power Station. Over the years the station utilised five 0-4-0 saddle tank locomotives, all built by Andrew Barclay of Kilmarnock. No.5 (W/No.2164 of 1944) was new to Clyde's Mill, and fitted with 14in x 22in outside cylinders. It was disused when photographed on 18 August 1970, standing on a rusty siding coupled to a similarly redundant hopper wagon. No.5 was scrapped about December 1971 and thereafter works shunting was left in the capable hands of two 0-4-0 diesel hydraulic locomotives (Andrew Barclay W/Nos.515 and 516 of 1966). The power station was later closed down and the plant and buildings demolished.

Moving further towards the southeast end of the city brings you to Motherwell, where the well-known Ravenscraig Iron & Steel Works was located. This massive integrated works had its own coking ovens, seen in this view dated 24 August 1980. Coke was produced in a battery of parallel ovens, seen in the left background. Each individual oven became ready for emptying in an ongoing cycle, whereupon a ram at the rear pushed the red hot coke out into the massive coke car wagon, which was correctly placed by the Robert Stephenson & Hawthorns 0-4-0 electric locomotive. The coke car was then positioned beneath the tall tower in the background and cold water sprayed onto the hot coke, sending vast plumes of steam up the tower. The coke car was then run forward and stopped and the side doors were opened, allowing the coke to pour down the 45 degrees slope into a wharf where it was collected and transported away by motor lorry.

A little further to the east of Motherwell is Wishaw, which is basically the south east extremity of Glasgow. Here was the works of R.Y. Pickering & Co Ltd, the manufacturer of rolling stock that will be well known to all wagon enthusiasts, and examples of whose diamond shape builder's plate will be in many a collection. On a sunny 2 July 1973, Pickering's yard was being shunted by the company's 100hp locomotive No.4, which was moving a single bogie tank wagon. Painted in the company's attractive standard maroon livery, this 4-wheel vertical boiler tank locomotive (Sentinel W/No.9559 of 1953) had front buffers with a small cut off section. No.4 had previously worked at the New Bilton Works, Rugby, of the Rugby Portland Cement Company. Nowadays it can be found preserved at the Tanfield Railway in County Durham.

On 2 July 1973, R.Y. Pickering & Co Ltd's veteran No.3 locomotive was standing disused on a siding, and also painted in the company's standard maroon livery. This 0-4-0 saddle tank was manufactured by R. & W. Hawthorn & Co of the Forth Bank Works at Newcastle upon Tyne (later Hawthorn Leslie), to the company's W/No.2009 of 1884. It was fitted with 12in x 19in outside cylinders and wheels of 3ft diameter. Built in England, this locomotive found its way to Wales, and there was rebuilt in 1937 by A.R. Adams Ltd of Newport, and then sold to R.Y. Pickering in Scotland. It will be noted that the worksplate is missing on the cab side, while the one higher up is a Railway Executive registration plate. Fortunately this old locomotive was saved for preservation and, like its old partner at Wishaw, nowadays can be found preserved at the Tanfield Railway in County Durham.

Also in Wishaw was the works of the Costain Concrete Co Ltd, which manufactured concrete railway sleepers, as seen on the extreme left of this picture. When visited on 12 June 1981, the company's inward rail traffic included steel reinforcement bars and rails, with prefabricated sections of BR track being despatched. The Hunslet Engine Company locomotive shown here (W/No.7430 of 1977) was a 4-wheel diesel hydraulic fitted with a 174hp engine, and was a most unusual beast. It had a motor on each axle coupled by a cardan shaft, twin headlights at front and rear, plus a small shunter's platform on each side at the front and a large full width platform behind the cab. It also had unusually large and strangely shaped buffers, to prevent buffer lock. Utilising its expertise, Costain had erected an unusual shed for the locomotive, a rounded structure made of pre-cast concrete sections.

The west coast of Scotland has never been renowned for its industrial railway systems and so the traveller from Dumbarton needed to pass Loch Lomond, Crianlarich and Glen Coe to reach the next location. This was the pulp and paper mill of Wiggins Teape Ltd, at Corpach, near Fort William. The works was officially opened on 15 September 1966, connected to BR's famous scenic line from Fort William to Mallaig. On 2 October 1984 the Wiggins Teape 'fleet' comprised ex-BR shunter 08077 (used five days per week) and 0-4-0 diesel hydraulic MARGARET (English Electric D1126 of 1966). MARGARET had been obtained in 1973 but by now was out of use with its 305hp engine removed. At this time BR delivered pulp, clay, oil tankers and empty wagons at 12.15pm, plus more pulp and clay at 6.15pm; finished paper was taken away at 1.05pm and empty oil tankers bound for Grangemouth at 3.00pm.

A decent length drive along the A82 and A87 roads leads the traveller in a north westerly direction to Kyle of Lochalsh, where a modern road bridge now leads over to the Isle of Skye. Kyle is the terminus of the famous scenic Highland line, and Inverness-bound travellers soon reach Stromeferry on the banks of Loch Carron. In connection with the offshore oil industry, in May 1975 Howard Doris Ltd brought two industrial locomotives to labour at its cement terminal in this far-flung outpost of the Scottish rail system. The company acquired 204hp 0-6-0 diesel mechanical D2007 TRIBRUIT (Hudswell Clarke W/No.D917 of 1956) and sister D2008 GUINNION (W/No.D918 of 1956), both being originally new to the Avonmouth Docks of the Port of Bristol Authority. When Stromeferry was visited on 21 August 1980, both locomotives were painted grey, fitted with a Gardner engine, and carried running numbers HD-LM1 and HD-LM2 respectively. GUINNION is seen here.

Any industrial railway enthusiast who was asked to discuss Scottish sites would be unlikely to mention the town of Invergordon. Yet the town once had two industrial railway locations of different gauges and, to boot, is the most northerly place featured in this book. When visited on 21 August 1980, the British Aluminium Company's Invergordon Works utilised a 4-wheel diesel mechanical 'Trackmobile' built (W/No.7505) by Strachan & Henshaw of Bristol. It was a model 4TMB, fitted with a four-speed gearbox, and equipped to operate on both road and rail. It was in fact one of the earliest examples of the road-railer type of vehicle, which nowadays are hugely popular and proliferate on all main line track-relaying contracts. It is seen here in road operating mode but, when it was positioned above railway track, hydraulic apparatus was activated, which allowed it to lower its rail wheels and undertake shunting.

In 1973 Key & Kramer Ltd installed a brand new 900mm gauge railway at its Invergordon Works. The company produced pipes for the off-shore oil industry and the narrow gauge system was an integral part of the production line. Three 4-wheel diesel hydraulic locomotives (Schöma W/Nos.3848/49/50 of 1973) were purchased via an agent in Rotterdam, and were of the maker's type CHL20G and fitted with a Deutz diesel engine of 2000rpm. The agent also supplied six long bogie wagons that were used to carry pipes and had a special sliding end section, which was positioned depending upon the length of pipe to be transported. Bare pipes rolled off a production line and were hoisted on to the wagons, whereupon a Schöma fed them into a spray plant, through which they were hauled by chain. A second Schöma then collected the wagons, and the pipes were offloaded and sent for concreting. When new, the system was used 24 hours per day, but when visited on 21 August 1980 the demand for pipes was not as great.

The main line from Invergordon runs south through Dingwall and Inverness, before heading in a south-easterly direction down to Aviemore. The last named town is the headquarters of the Strathspey Railway, which was originally formed with the intention (subsequently realised) of operating trains to Boat of Garten. Back on 4 October 1984, a visit to the Railway's headquarters in the former BR Aviemore steam shed produced fourteen ex industrial locomotives standing in the sidings. Amongst these was dismantled 0-6-0 side tank No.17 (Andrew Barclay W/No.2017 of 1935) which was fitted with 18in x 26in inside cylinders and 4ft 3in diameter wheels. It was originally new to the Wemyss Coal Co Ltd in Fife and remained on that company's system (including after nationalisation) all its working life. Late in 1970 it moved to scrap merchant T. Muir of Thornton, from where it subsequently moved to Aviemore.

The Kingdom of Fife was once a major centre of the coal industry, with many collieries and workshops, plus several coal-shipping ports. Frances Colliery at Dysart was sunk on Blair Point by the Earl of Rosslyn's Collieries Ltd. Production commenced in 1878, with most of the coal workings beneath the adjacent Firth of Forth. It was taken over by the Fife Coal Company in 1923, and the NCB in 1947. Coal was sent out via a standard gauge branch line that ran westwards from the pit, crossing the A955 road en-route, to join the BR line running northwards out of Kirkcaldy. On 16 August 1972 veteran 0-4-0 saddle tank No.29 (Andrew Barclay W/No.1142 of 1908) was working the pit sidings. It was fitted with 14in x 22in outside cylinders. The use of steam continued into the 1980s, but the pit never resumed production after the infamous 1984/85 miners' strike, and eventually closed.

A couple of miles north of Dysart, midway between Kirkcaldy and Glenrothes, is the village of Thornton. Back in the days of main line BR steam, Thornton was much visited by railway enthusiasts due to the existence of shed 62A where, even up to the mid 1960s, working WD, J36 and J38 locomotives could still be seen in action. The village was also the base for scrap merchant T. Muir, which established its yard at Easter Balbeggie. In addition to its run of the mill scrap activities, at one time Muir's accumulated a collection of redundant ex-NCB steam locomotives, which were not cut up, but for years remained stored in the yard. Such was the case on 23 August 1980 when 0-4-0 saddle tank No.3 (Andrew Barclay 946 of 1902) was found languishing amongst the weeds. This 14in x 22in locomotive is still in Muir ownership, but now transferred to the company's yard on Den Road at Kirkcaldy.

Leaving Dysart, following the Fife coast westwards through Kirkcaldy and Kinghorn brings you to the small town of Burntisland, whose first coal dock opened in 1876. The British Aluminium Company set up its works at the west end of the town, alongside the main line from Inverkeithing. At its works the company utilised a 2ft 0in gauge railway, but was best known for its superb steam-operated standard gauge system, which the BACo was always willing to allow enthusiasts to visit. The company used three steam locomotives, which were all purchased new for the Burntisland Works and always maintained in excellent condition. On 16 August 1972, the company's oldest locomotive (Peckett W/No.1376 of 1915) was standing outside the shed, and by then out of use. Fortunately it was saved for preservation and nowadays can be seen at the Caledonian Railway at Brechin.

In addition to Peckett 1376, the British Aluminium Company used two other steam locomotives at its Burntisland Works. Of these, one was Peckett W/No.1579 of 1921, an 0-4-0 saddle tank fitted with 10in x 15in outside cylinders and 2ft 9in diameter wheels, the same as partner 1376. The third and final steamer was built by Andrew Barclay of Kilmarnock (W/No.2046 of 1937) and was an 0-4-0 saddle tank fitted with 10in x 18in outside cylinders. On a visit of 3 July 1973, the Barclay was found in action in the sidings, its green livery looking a little work worn but still master of its job. Although it was working on this date, 2046's status was that of standby since the arrival of diesels in 1971, and it was mostly stored in the shed. It was later saved for preservation, and these days can be seen at the Bo'ness headquarters of the Scottish Railway Preservation Society's Bo'ness & Kinneil Railway.

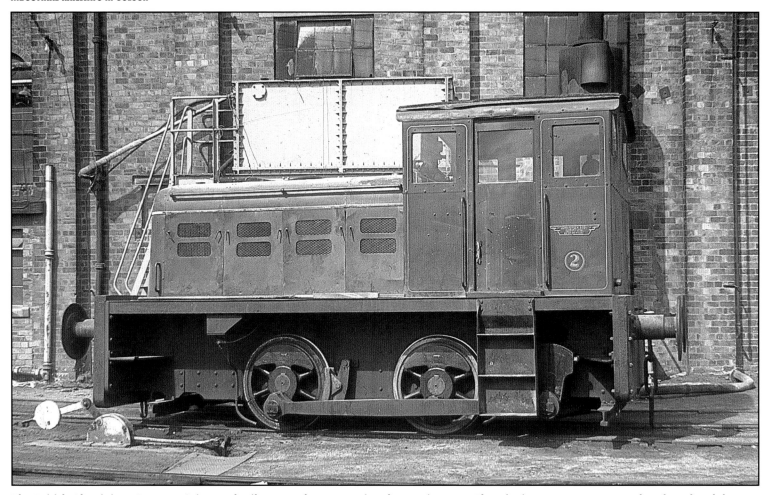

The British Aluminium Company's internal railways underwent major changes in 1971. The 2ft 0in gauge system was abandoned and the two Ruston & Hornsby 4-wheel diesel mechanical locomotives both went for scrap to the Thornton yard of T. Muir. On the standard gauge, two diesels arrived about November 1971 from United Fireclay Products Ltd of Armadale in West Lothian. The pair were 0-4-0 diesel mechanicals manufactured by John Fowler of Leeds (W/Nos.4210004 of 1949 and 4210045 of 1951) and equipped with a 150hp engine, four speed mechanical gearbox, and with final drive by jackshaft and side rods. The 421 Class proved to be an extremely popular design from Fowlers and (built between 1949 and 1959) became a common sight at various locations all over the UK. On a visit of 16 August 1972, Fowler W/No.4210045 was standing in the sidings between duties.

Almost due north of Burntisland, just west of Kirkcaldy, is the small town of Cardenden in Fife. It was a mining village with Bowhill Nos.1, 2 and 3 collieries, acquired in 1947 by the NCB from the Fife Coal Company. The pit sidings were at the terminus of the eastern arm of the Glencraig & Bowhill Colliery Branch (BR) three quarters of a mile north-west of Cardenden village. The colliery closed on 15 July 1965 but the coal preparation plant remained in use. Standing outside the brick-built locomotive shed on 20 May 1977 was 0-6-0 diesel hydraulic No.6 (North British W/No.27591 of 1957) which was fitted with a NBL/MAN engine rated at 440hp, Voith transmission, and jackshaft drive. It was supplied new to Wellesley Colliery and moved to Bowhill CPP in September 1969, going to the Kilmarnock Works of Andrew Barclay for overhaul in September 1974.

The National Coal Board maintained a series of central workshop facilities throughout the United Kingdom. The theory was that, rather than every individual colliery trying to be a jack-of-all-trades, a central workshop would service a group of pits and provide specialist skills, workmen and machinery. In Fife such workshops were provided at Cowdenbeath and Dysart. As regards locomotives, routine maintenance and smaller repairs were usually carried out at individual collieries, sometimes utilising spares that were sent from the central workshops. When major overhauls were required, locomotives went to the central facility. On 19 May 1977 a visit to Cowdenbeath Workshops revealed Andrew Barclay 0-4-0 saddle tanks No.47 (W/No.2157 of 1943) and No.29 (W/No.1142 of 1908) awaiting a decision on their futures. Both were fitted with 14in x 22in outside cylinders.

Heading south from Cowdenbeath soon brings the traveller to the world famous road and rail bridges, which cross the Firth of Forth between Inverkeithing (on the north bank) and Queensferry on the south. At Inverkeithing (still within the county of Fife) was the shipbreaking yard of Thos. W. Ward Ltd, the well known merchant with scrap yards all around the United Kingdom. On 1 June 1978 a long wooden display board was inspected in the main hallway of the office block, listing all the ships broken up at Inverkeithing since 1922. Over the years a number of steam locomotives were used to shunt the yard but, by the 1970s, diesels had taken over. Shunting a rake of 16 ton mineral wagons was yellow livery John Fowler W/ No.4220003 of 1959, an 0-4-0 diesel hydraulic fitted with a 176hp engine with final drive by jackshaft and side rods.

Upon leaving Inverkeithing, a short drive westwards along the north bank of the Firth of Forth brings you to Rosyth. Here was the Ministry of Defence (Navy Department) Royal Naval Dockyard, which produced a somewhat unexpected welcome when visited on 1 June 1978. Although having obtained, in writing, advance permission for a visit, the author's official documentation was treated with total contempt by the MoD gatemen. These over-zealous, sceptical and surly men interrogated and frisked the author, searched his camera bag, car interior and boot, and made several lengthy internal telephone calls, before reluctantly and dismissively allowing entry when the pre-arranged and briefed Naval guide arrived on the scene. Somewhat chastened, the author was then allowed to photograph the dockyard's two 'Planet' 4-wheel diesel mechanical locomotives, with three-speed gearbox, of which YARD No.2868 (Hibberd W/No.3739 of 1955) is seen here.

To the north-west of Rosyth, beyond Dunfermline, was the village of Saline in Fife. Close by was Comrie Colliery, originally operated by the Fife Coal Co Ltd before being taken over by the NCB in 1947. It was connected to BR by a quite scenic two mile branch that joined the Alloa-Dunfermline main line at exchange sidings west of Oakley Station. In the mid-1970s the colliery still used steam power and was notable for simultaneously operating a pair of relatively rare giesl ejector fitted 0-6-0 saddle tanks. By 31 May 1978, however, the colliery had hired shunter 08425 from BR and the two giesl locomotives were standing in the yard. On the left is No.5 (Hunslet Engine Company W/No.3837 of 1955) and on the right No.7 (Bagnall W/No.2777 of 1945).

On visits to collieries it was relatively rare to be able to photograph underground locomotives because – of course – they were usually deep beneath the earth! On certain occasions, however, such machines emerged and could be found 'up top', usually undergoing repair. They might also be put to work on the surface, like here at Comrie Colliery on 31 May 1978 where this small 0-4-0 diesel mechanical flameproof locomotive (Hunslet W/No.3200 of 1946) is stabled between duties. It was originally built to an order placed on 10 September 1943 by the Fife Coal Company and delivered to Comrie Colliery on 5 February 1946, for coal haulage underground. It was a 2ft 8in gauge machine, fitted with a Gardner four-cylinder engine rated at 50hp, two-speed gearbox, wheels of 1ft 8½in diameter, and final drive by jackshaft (between the wheels) and coupling rods.

Moving south-west out of Fife and over the Kincardine Bridge, brings you to the small town of Stenhousemuir, which is probably best known for its weekly appearances over the airwaves when the football results are read out! Carbrook Mine was located near the town, on the edge of Tor Wood, and opened in 1953 by Graigend Refractories Ltd to work for fireclay. When visited on 11 June 1981, the mine's average production was 65 tons of fireclay per day, which was mined 300 feet below ground and one mile distant from the portal. Thirteen men were employed and the fireclay was brought out of the mine in a fleet of over sixty 2ft 0in gauge tubs, which Graigend Refractories had purchased second-hand from the National Coal Board. A rake is being pulled up the 1 in 3 incline out of the mine by a stationary LDC electric haulage engine. By July 1995 the mine had been closed and the site cleared.

To the south of Stenhousemuir was the village of Longriggend, where Richardsons Moss Litter Company once operated its Fannyside Works. When visited on 25 August 1980 the company owned a fleet of sixteen operational wooden wagons, and peat was brought in off the moss in rakes of four. These were hauled by a 2ft 6in gauge 4-wheel diesel mechanical locomotive built by Lister Blackstone Rail Traction Ltd of Dursley in Gloucestershire (W/No.55870) and which was new to Fannyside in 1968. In order to work efficiently on lightweight track across a spongy peat bog, this locomotive was of as basic a design as it is possible to get: a lightweight chassis upon which was mounted a two-cylinder Lister diesel engine, a brake handle, and a moulded driver's seat which was open to the elements. On this date, the driver was Allison Patterson, a former art student who had given up her course to work full-time as a locomotive driver!

A few miles south-east of Longriggend was Polkemmet Colliery in the parish of Whitburn, West Lothian, near to the present-day M8 motorway. Sinking of the colliery by William Dixon & Company commenced early in World War 1, but problems due to the hostilities meant that it was not fully operational until mid-1923. Its principal product was high quality coking coal, mainly used in Lanarkshire steel works. During the 1950s it was extensively reconstructed, after which it produced an average of over 2,000 tons of coal per day. The colliery was famed for its steam locomotives but, on a visit of 24 August 1980, a 4-wheel vertical boiler steam crane was also to be seen. This was constructed (W/No.2485) by Grafton Cranes Ltd of the Vulcan Works in Bedford.

Polkemmet Colliery's coal was sent out via a steeply graded line from the colliery yard up to exchange sidings on Polkemmet Moor. From there a mineral branch ran across the moor to Benhar Junction (connecting with the ex CR/LMS Edinburgh-Glasgow line) and to the former NBR/LNER Bathgate-Morningside line (closed 1964). The line up to Polkemmet exchange sidings was very steep and so, on a daily basis, the coal trains were double-headed. On average eight 300-ton coal trains a day were worked up the bank, and enthusiasts flocked to watch the spectacle. On a very gloomy 2 June 1976, two Andrew Barclay 0-6-0 saddle tanks are beginning the climb up from the colliery, with the screens and headgears visible in the background. Leading is veteran Andrew Barclay No.8 (W/No.1175 of 1909) with the more modern No.25 (W/No.2358 of 1954) tucked in behind.

Having battled to the top of the gradient, the loaded coal wagons were left in the sidings for collection by BR, whilst the colliery engines coupled on to empties which were taken down-grade and left on the inclined screens roads, as seen in the previous picture. After a shunter with brake pole had lowered them through the screens for filling with coal, the wagons were marshalled together and collected on the low side of the screens by the double-header steamers, in a cycle that continued day after day. On 1 June 1978 a pair of Andrew Barclay locomotives were again in action, now at the very start of their attack on the bank. Leading is 0-6-0 saddle tank No.25 (W/No.2358 of 1954) with giesl-fitted 0-6-0 side tank No.8 (W/No.1296 of 1912) coupled behind. Steam working finished in the summer of 1980 and thereafter 350hp class 08 diesel-electric shunters were hired from BR.

0-6-0 saddle tank No.25 was in action on 1 June 1978 (in the previous illustration) but is now between duties on the same day, posing for its portrait to be taken. Loaded coal wagons can just be glimpsed in the right background, which No.25 was about to collect. No.25 was built at the Caledonia Works in Kilmarnock of Andrew Barclay, Sons & Co Ltd (W/No.2358) in 1954. It was fitted with 16in x 24in outside cylinders and carries two plates on its cab side: the lower is its Barclay works plate, and the upper is a British Transport Commission (3066 of 1964) registration plate, which showed that the locomotive had been checked by BTC personnel and passed for running on BR metals in the exchange sidings area. A tiny third plate reading BL39 cannot be made out in this view. No.25 is now preserved at the Scottish Industrial Railway Centre at Dalmellington in Ayrshire.

An earlier picture (page 58) saw No.8 (Andrew Barclay W/No.1175 of 1909) in action at Polkemmet Colliery on 2 June 1976; here it is on 1 June 1978, standing in the yard near the locomotive shed in the traditional Polkemmet livery of ground-in grime! It was an 0-6-0 saddle tank fitted with 15in x 20in outside cylinders and was originally new to Arniston Colliery at Gorebridge. After over forty years faithful service there, it moved to Lady Victoria Colliery about 1953, and arrived at Polkemmet Colliery about March 1973. It was saved for preservation by West Lothian Council and can now be seen at Polkemmet Country Park, having been named DARDANELLES. The underground workings at Polkemmet flooded during the 1984/85 miners' strike and the pit never worked again, officially closing in June 1986.

The shed at Polkemmet Colliery on 17 August 1977. Taking water on the left is No.8, with bright yellow coal bunker (Barclay W/No.1296 of 1912). It is an 0-6-0 side tank fitted with 18in x 24in outside cylinders and 3ft 7in diameter wheels. On the right is No.25 (Andrew Barclay W/No.2358 of 1954) an 0-6-0 saddle tank fitted with 16in x 24in outside cylinders. No.8 was of interest, with the NCB willing to finance its costly overhaul and repaint at Cowdenbeath Central Workshops as late as 1971. The pristine veteran was then put to work at Bedlay Colliery and, after a few years there, it found its way to Polkemmet Colliery. Nowadays it can be seen at the Scottish Industrial Railway Centre at Dalmellington. The interesting display of dismantled parts in the foreground includes the inverted cab and works plate of Andrew Barclay W/No.885 of 1900.

Kinneil Colliery was on the south bank of the Firth of Forth at Bo'ness in West Lothian. Numerous pits were sunk in the area over the years, and Kinneil was actually a redevelopment (from June 1951) in the yard of Furnaceyard Colliery, in search of high quality coking coal. In April 1964, after eighteen months of digging, Kinneil was linked by a 3½ miles tunnel beneath the Forth to Valleyfield Colliery in Fife, and thereafter most of the production from the two pits was raised and processed at Kinneil's preparation plant. On 20 May 1977 the yard was being energetically shunted by 0-4-0 saddle tank No.6 (Andrew Barclay W/No.2043 of 1937) which was fitted with 16in x 24in outside cylinders and an open-back cab. Kinneil Colliery closed in 1982, and No.6 later worked at Bedlay Colliery, although it is now preserved at East Lothian District Council's Prestongrange Mining Museum at Prestonpans.

Heading away from Kinneil the A1 passes through Edinburgh and leads eastwards across to the coastal town of Dunbar, and the cement works of Associated Portland Cement Manufacturers Ltd (later Blue Circle Ltd). Its Oxwellmains Cement Works was alongside, and connected to, the East Coast Main Line. The works had been shunted by diesels from the early 1960s and, on a visit of 6 October 1991, the roster comprised a quartet of 4-wheel diesel hydraulics built by Sentinel of Shrewsbury. Double-heading a rake of cement tankers are W/Nos.10266 of 1967 and 10021 of 1959. The works is still operational and in early 2006 had eight Sentinels, albeit with several disused and dismantled for spares. And so our clockwise tour of Scotland ends, as we drive out of Dunbar, pick up the A1 and head south, crossing the border just to the north of Berwick upon Tweed.